**Genre** Biogra...

MW00682108

 Essential Question
What impact do our actions have on our world?

Marjory Stoneman Douglas

GUARDIAN OF THE EVERGLADES

BY JANE KELLEY

Introduction 2

Chapter 1
Early Life 3

Chapter 2
A River of Grass 7

Chapter 3
Fighting On. 10

Conclusion. 14

Respond to Reading 15

PAIRED READ The Story of the Tree Musketeers. . . 16

Glossary/Index 19

STEM Focus on Science .20

Introduction

The Everglades in southern Florida were given that name because the glades, or grassy places, seemed to go on forever. Water flowed all across the area as well. The ground was too wet for crops or buildings. Many people looked at this landscape and saw a useless swamp.

Writer Marjory Stoneman Douglas could see the rich variety of life in the Everglades and how the place was different from anywhere else. She described its beauty: "The miracle of the light pours over the green and brown expanse of saw grass and of water, shining and slow-moving below."

This area in the Everglades is called a freshwater prairie.

CHAPTER ONE

Early Life

Douglas's writings about the Everglades influenced many people. How did she end up writing about the Everglades? She never spent a lot of time outdoors. She wasn't even from Florida, although she had happy memories of a trip to Tampa when she was a child.

Marjory was born in Minneapolis on April 7, 1890. Most of her childhood was spent in Massachusetts. She spent lots of time in libraries and loved discovering things in books. Gradually she gained the research skills she would use in her work as a writer.

This photograph shows Marjory when she was just one and a half years old.

Marjory studied at Wellesley College. In her senior year, she was editor of the college yearbook. She was the class orator because she was good at giving speeches.

Marjory attended Wellesley College in Massachusetts.

After she graduated in 1912, Marjory didn't know what to do next. She took a job in a department store in Newark, New Jersey. She taught basic grammar and math skills to the sales clerks.

Marjory was married to Kenneth Douglas for less than two years. When her marriage ended in 1915, she moved to Miami, Florida, where her father lived.

Douglas's father, Frank Stoneman, was editor-in-chief of *The Miami Herald*. He hired his daughter to write the newspaper's society column. Douglas was thrilled to be writing. Her father also told her about his passion for saving Miami's older neighborhoods and the area west of the city called the Everglades.

Douglas's father, Frank Stoneman, hired her as a writer.

When World War I started, Douglas joined the Red Cross. The Red Cross needed staff and volunteers to help relieve the suffering caused by the war. From Europe Douglas wrote about the work of the Red Cross and urged people to support its efforts. She also saw the plight of refugees who had to leave their homes after the war. As a result, Douglas was sympathetic to people in trouble.

World War I ended in 1918. When Douglas came back in 1920, Miami had four times as many people as before. The city needed more land. Much of the nearby land was part of the Everglades. **Developers** dug canals to drain the **wetlands**. Most of them didn't think about the native animals and plants living in the wetlands.

Douglas became *The Miami Herald*'s assistant editor. She wrote a column about the big issues of the time. She knew from her work during the war that decent living conditions were important. She wrote about women's rights. She also urged that the Everglades be protected as a national park.

Draining the wetlands affected the animals and plants living there.

STOP AND CHECK

What were the issues that Douglas wrote about?

CHAPTER TWO

A River of Grass

Douglas worked hard on the newspaper. She also started **campaigns** to help people, such as one to provide milk for poor families.

In 1924, she quit the newspaper and wrote short stories instead. She sold her stories to magazines. However, she never forgot the social issues that were important to her.

This great egret was photographed in the Everglades.

Even though some of her stories won awards, Douglas couldn't always sell her work. Sometimes it was hard for her to earn a living.

Then in 1941, her friend Hervey Allen asked her to write a book about the Miami River.

Douglas didn't want to write about the Miami River. She suggested to Hervey Allen that she write a book about the Everglades instead. Allen agreed and said he would publish the book when it was finished.

Douglas got right to work. She used her skills as a reporter to research the area. She interviewed people and wrote about topics ranging from the Native Americans who lived there to the **geology** of the Everglades.

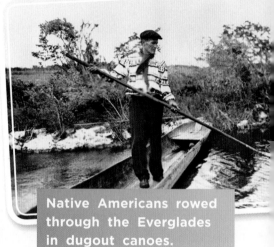

Native Americans rowed through the Everglades in dugout canoes.

Then Douglas found a new way to describe the Everglades. It changed how people thought about them. She said she saw the Everglades as a glistening "river of grass."

In her book, Douglas said the Everglades were unlike any other place in the world:

> They are ... one of the unique regions of the earth, remote, never wholly known. Nothing anywhere else is like them; their vast glittering openness, wider than the enormous visible round of the horizon, the racing free saltness and sweetness of their massive winds, under the dazzling blue heights of space.

Why did she say the Everglades are unique? Look at the large lake in the center of the map. Water flows south from the lake across a bed of limestone. Sawgrass grows on top of the limestone. This kind of water flow isn't found anywhere else in the world.

Douglas was right: The Everglades are a river of grass. The river is dotted with islands of higher ground.

THE ECOSYSTEM

The Everglades have many habitats. Each habitat is home to a group of living things that depend on one another and the environment. Together the habitats form the Everglades ecosystem.

If the temperature isn't right or there isn't enough food or water, then the ecosystem could collapse.

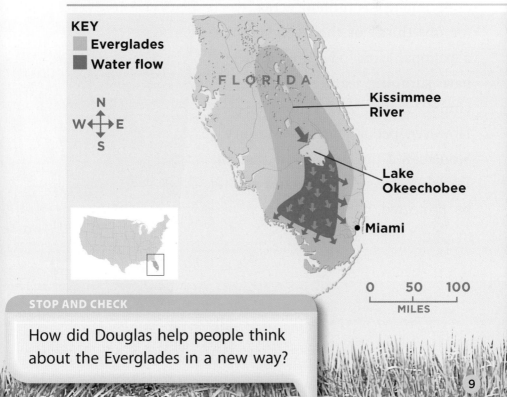

WATER FLOW THROUGH THE EVERGLADES

KEY
Everglades
Water flow

N
W E
S

FLORIDA

Kissimmee River

Lake Okeechobee

• Miami

0   50   100
MILES

STOP AND CHECK

How did Douglas help people think about the Everglades in a new way?

CHAPTER THREE

Fighting On

The Everglades: River of Grass was published in 1947. It sold 7,500 copies in one month. Readers liked the way Douglas explained people's connection to this special place. The river of grass was nourishing the plants and animals. It also provided people with water. If the Everglades were drained, water wouldn't flow into the **aquifers** underneath the sawgrass. Southern Florida would become a semitropical desert.

President Truman set aside about 1.5 million acres (or one-third) of the Everglades as a national park. The area didn't have stunning features like the Grand Canyon and Yellowstone. However, people such as Marjory Stoneman Douglas showed that the Everglades were unique and should be protected.

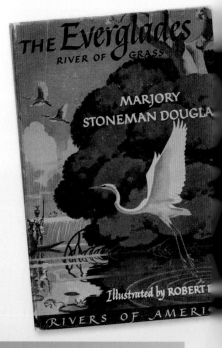

This is the original cover of Douglas's book.

Douglas was in awe of the Everglades, but she didn't find it welcoming. She said, "... it's too buggy, too wet, too generally inhospitable."

Douglas also wrote other nonfiction books about Florida. Two were for younger readers, *Freedom River* and *Alligator Crossing*. She was often asked to speak about her most famous book.

Some of the Everglades area was protected by the national park, but the rest was still at risk. The owners of sugar plantations wanted to control the water so they could grow more sugarcane. Developers wanted more dry land to build housing. Canals were dug to drain water away from the marshes.

Douglas played an important role in saving the Florida Everglades.

In 1969, developers wanted to build an airport in the Everglades. Joe Browder, a TV reporter who was also an **environmentalist**, asked Douglas to help him stop the airport. She started a group called Friends of the Everglades and spoke out against the airport project.

People paid attention, and the airport wasn't built. However, Douglas said the water in the Everglades needed to be restored. She asked that polluters clean up the water and get rid of the canals that took water away from the area.

PROTECTING OTHER WETLANDS

All around the world, people see that they need to protect the wetlands in their communities. In 1990, Rosa Hilda Ramos formed Communities United Against Contamination in San Juan, the capital of Puerto Rico.

The group got companies to clean up pollution and pay fines. The money from fines was used to buy Las Cucharillas Marsh. This wetland is a safe place for birds and people.

This bird is hunting for food in Las Cucharillas Marsh.

Douglas never lost her fighting spirit. She spoke out in the early 1980s when developers threatened the Everglades again.

She was in her 90s and wore thick glasses because her vision was poor. But Sam Poole, who worked for the South Florida Water Management District, said she stood her ground in front of the hostile crowd. "She cast a giant shadow over the Everglades," he said. "One small person can make a difference. She made a huge difference."

Douglas received many awards. One was the Medal of Freedom. The citation said her work "enhanced our nation's respect for our precious environment."

From what threats did Douglas try to protect the Everglades?

President Clinton presented Douglas with the Medal of Freedom.

13

Douglas wanted to save the plants and animals in the Everglades.

Conclusion

The Everglades Forever Act was passed in 1994. Its purpose was to save and restore the water needed by plants and animals that live in the Everglades.

Douglas knew that people's support was also needed to protect the Everglades. So she founded the Young Friends of the Everglades. "Take the children out to the Glades and let them learn," Douglas said. "Education will be the only way to save the Glades."

In 1997, 1.3 million acres of the Everglades were named the Marjory Stoneman Douglas Wilderness. Douglas died in 1998, aged 108. Her books and her life still inspire anyone who wants to help the environment.

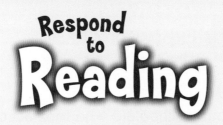

Respond to Reading

Summarize

Use the most important details from the text to summarize the biography of Marjory Stoneman Douglas. Your graphic organizer may help you.

Problem	Solution

Text Evidence

1. How can you tell that this text is a biography? Give examples from the text to support your answer. GENRE

2. Why did Douglas think draining the wetlands was a problem on page 10? What did she think the solution might be? PROBLEM AND SOLUTION

3. What is the meaning of *inhospitable* on page 11? Use clues in the paragraph to figure it out. Find a nearby antonym that can also help you figure out the meaning. SYNONYMS AND ANTONYMS

4. Write about how Douglas helped the Everglades and the people of Florida. Give examples of the problems she faced and the actions she took to solve them. WRITE ABOUT READING

Compare Texts
Read about a schoolgirl who took action
by planting trees.

The Story of the Tree Musketeers

In 1987, there was a drought in California. Tara
Church was eight years old, and her scout troop was
going camping. Tara's mom asked the girls to choose
between paper and tin plates. Paper plates didn't need to
be washed and would save water. However, paper comes
from trees. Tin plates would save trees. The girls talked
about the plates, and they decided to plant more trees.

Tin camping plates save trees.
Campers can also reduce waste
by reusing utensils.

Trees are an important resource. Their roots help soil stay in place. Trees also make oxygen and help clean the air. They provide food and shelter for other living things.

Tara and her friends planted their first tree on Imperial Avenue in El Segundo, California. They named it Marcie the Marvelous Tree.

The children planted more trees and persuaded other scout groups to do the same. They called themselves the Tree Musketeers after the book *The Three Musketeers*.

Their organization grew. People liked it because it was run by children. Kids taught other kids how to help the environment. Kids learned how to plant trees and take care of them, and how to get more kids to take part.

In 1988, the Tree Musketeers went to Washington, D.C., to receive an environmental youth award.

The work of the Tree Musketeers was ready to export to other countries. The group began to exchange ideas with chapters all over the world. Today Tara and her friends are too old to be members of the Tree Musketeers. However, their efforts got many more kids working to help the environment.

The group has projects such as the One in a Million tree-planting program and Partners for the Planet. These projects encourage kids to protect the natural world.

Marcie the Marvelous Tree is more than 50 feet tall now. It is still helping to cool the city, clean the air, and inspire kids to make a difference.

Planting trees is an easy way for kids to help the environment in their communities.

Make Connections

Why do you think Tara's ideas have spread so far around the world? ESSENTIAL QUESTION

Compare Douglas in *Marjory Stoneman Douglas: Guardian of the Everglades* with Tara in *The Story of the Tree Musketeers*. How are they alike? How are they different? TEXT TO TEXT

Glossary

aquifers *(A-kwuh-fuhrz)* layers of soil or rock that can store water *(page 10)*

campaigns *(kam-PAYNZ)* organized actions to bring about change *(page 7)*

developers *(di-VEL-uh-puhrz)* business people that build houses or other structures *(page 6)*

environmentalist *(in-vigh-ruhn-MEN-tuhl-ist)* a person who helps protect the environment *(page 12)*

geology *(jee-AH-luh-jee)* the rocks and other materials that make up Earth *(page 8)*

wetlands *(WET-landz)* areas soaked with water, such as swamps *(page 6)*

Index

Allen, Hervey, *7, 8*

Church, Tara, *16–18*

Everglades Forever Act, *14*

Everglades: River of Grass, The, 10

Friends of the Everglades, *12*

Marjory Stoneman Douglas Wilderness, *14*

Red Cross, *5*

Stoneman, Frank, *5*

Tree Musketeers, *16–18*

Young Friends of the Everglades, *14*

Focus on Science

Purpose To learn about threats to your local environment and to take action

Procedure

Step 1 With a partner or group, research local environmental problems, such as getting people to recycle, cleaning up a trash-filled park, or stopping the pollution of a river or stream.

Step 2 Choose one of the problems you would like to help with. Check with your teacher to make sure it's not dangerous. Identify the cause or causes of the problem. Suggest something people could do to help, such as removing trash.

Step 3 With the help of your teacher and other adults, plan a work day at the site. What supplies will you need? How will you let people in your community know what you're doing?

Step 4 After you've had your work day, report back to the class. What did you do? How was the site restored?

Conclusion How was the environment improved by your actions? What else needs to be done?